LET'S COOK

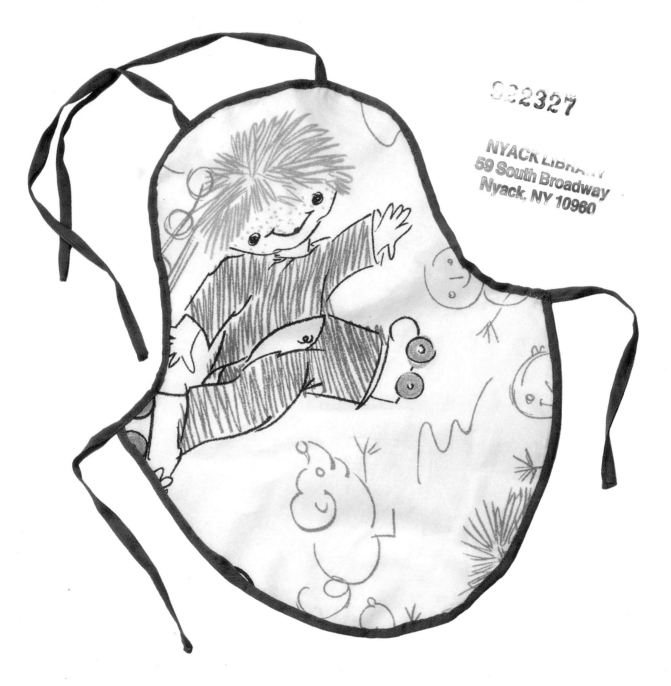

Dr. Oetker

 Sterling Publishing Co., Inc.   New York

Library of Congress Cataloging-in-Publication Data

Kinder Kochbuch. English.
   Let's cook / Dr. Oetker ; [translated by Annette Englander].
      p. cm.
   Translation of: Kinder Kochbuch.
   Includes index.
   Summary: Presents a variety of recipes for snacks, main dishes,
desserts, and beverages.
   ISBN 0-8069-8532-1
   1. Cookery—Juvenile literature. [1. Cookery.] I. Englander,
Annette. II. Dr. Oetker (Firm). III. Title.
TX652.5.K48713   1992
641.5—dc20   91-46336
                                                     CIP
                                                      AC

10 9 8 7 6 5 4 3 2 1

Translated by Annette Englander

English translation © 1992 by Sterling Publishing Company
387 Park Avenue South, New York, N.Y. 10016
Original edition published under the title
Kinder Kochbuch © 1990 by Ceres Verlag and
Rudolf-August-Oetker KG, Bielefeld
Distributed in Canada by Sterling Publishing
% Canadian Manda Group, P.O. Box 920, Station U
Toronto, Ontario, Canada M8Z 5P9
Distributed in Great Britain and Europe by Cassell PLC
Villiers House, 41/47 Strand, London WC2N 5JE
Distributed in Australia by Capricorn Link Ltd.
P.O. Box 665, Lane Cove, NSW 2066
Printed in Hong Kong
All rights reserved

Sterling ISBN   0-8069-8532-1

Noodles

Homemade
Noodles 23

Spaghetti with
Meat Sauce 24

Easy Cheese
Noodles 25

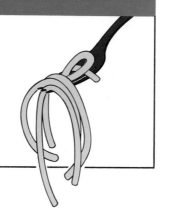

Vegetables

Fruited Cabbage
Salad 27

Egg Mushrooms in
Spinach Bed 31

Tomato-Cucumber
Boats 28

Broccoli Cake 29

Fruits

Crunchy Apple
Dish 33

Apple Soup with
Kiwi 34

Fruit Salad 34

Beverages

Pineapple-Yogurt
Shake 36

Tingly Orange
Punch 40

Apricot Flip 37

Banana
Milkshake 41

Hot Spiced
Cup 38

Lemon Tea 39

Measurement abbreviations used:

Common	Metric
qt = quart	cm = centimetre
lb = pound	g = gram
oz = ounce	kg = kilogram
pkg = package	L = litre
t = teaspoon	mL = millilitre
T = tablespoon	

Birthday

Baked Banana
Boats 43

Pizza Napoli 46

Honeyspice
Cookies 44

Index 48

Kitchen Utensils

Skewers

Sieve (s

Skimming Ladle

Whisk

Mixer (knead hooks)

Colander

Measuring Cup

Carving Kni

Grater

Puréer/Blender

Kit

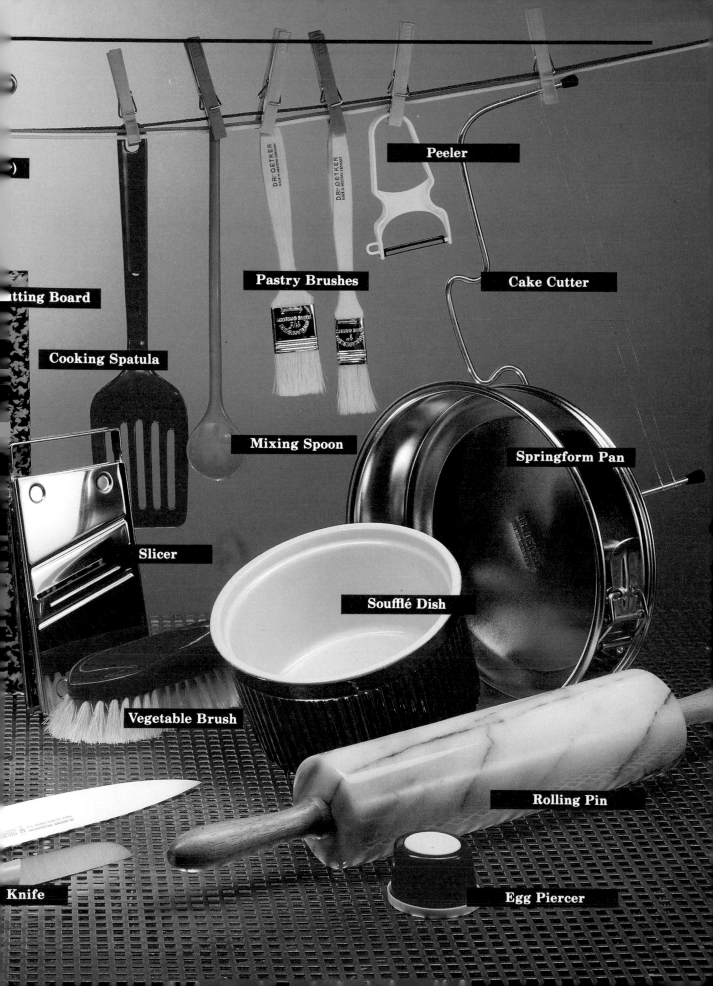

Peeler

Pastry Brushes

Cake Cutter

tting Board

Cooking Spatula

Mixing Spoon

Springform Pan

Slicer

Soufflé Dish

Vegetable Brush

Rolling Pin

Knife

Egg Piercer

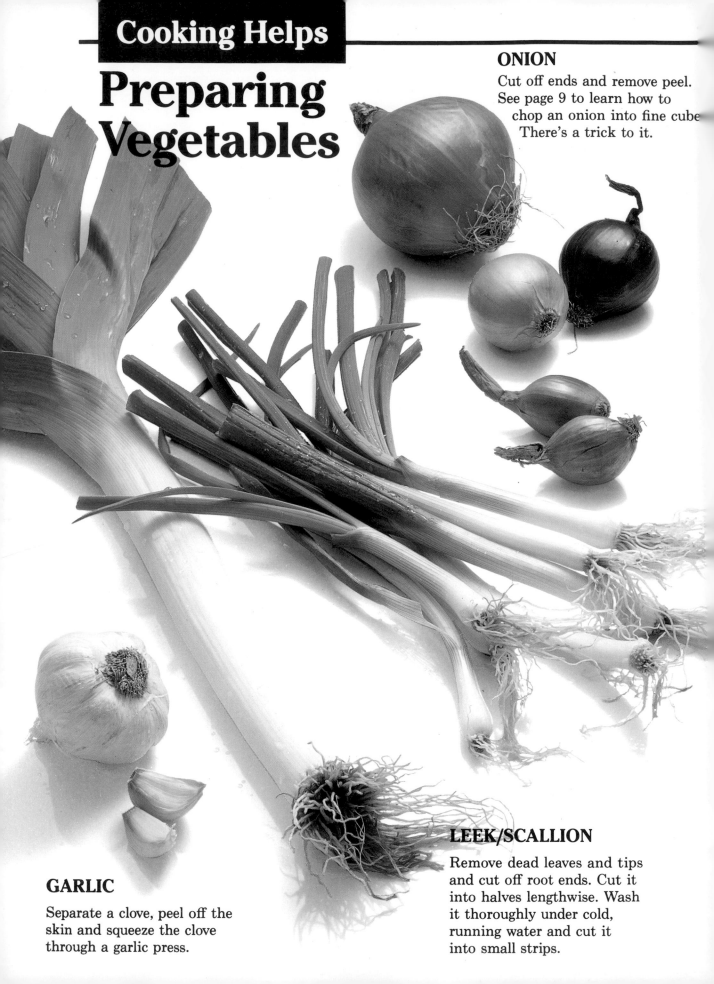

Preparing Vegetables

ONION

Cut off ends and remove peel. See page 9 to learn how to chop an onion into fine cube There's a trick to it.

GARLIC

Separate a clove, peel off the skin and squeeze the clove through a garlic press.

LEEK/SCALLION

Remove dead leaves and tips and cut off root ends. Cut it into halves lengthwise. Wash it thoroughly under cold, running water and cut it into small strips.

CUCUMBER

Wash cucumber thoroughly under warm, running water. You don't need to peel it. Slice it with a kitchen knife or slicer.

ZUCCHINI

Wash the zucchini thoroughly under warm, running water and cut off both ends. This squash can be sliced or cubed for salad, or cut into sticks to eat with dip.

PEPPER

Cut it in half. Remove the stem, seeds, and the white inside walls, which are very bitter. Wash the pepper under cold, running water. Cut it into cubes or thin slices.

EGGPLANT

Wash the eggplant under cold, running water, then remove both ends with a knife. Recipes usually call for eggplant to be sliced.

TOMATO

Wash it under cold, running water and remove the stem. Cut it into slices, quarters, or large cubes.

Cooking Tips To Help You

1. Before you begin to cook, put on an apron or kitchen towel to protect your clothing. When you work with them, some foods will "squirt," and stains from the juice of red berries, for example, are very difficult to remove.

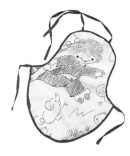

2. Always wash your hands before working with food.

3. Read the recipe that you want to prepare carefully all the way through first.

4. Ask an adult to show you how to operate the stove and oven you will be using and to stay nearby in case you need help while you are learning.

5. Make sure you have all the measured ingredients and utensils you will need before you start the recipe.

6. While learning, follow the quantities given in the recipe exactly, so that they will turn out okay. Later, you can experiment and make changes.

7. You can use a kitchen scale to weigh large amounts of flour, fruits, and other ingredients for recipes, but don't forget to subtract the weight of the bowl in which you weighed them!

8. Small quantities are given in tablespoons (T) and teaspoons (t). Metric measurements of ingredients are provided only for larger amounts.

9. Very small quantities are measured with a pinch. A pinch is as much as you can hold between your thumb and your forefinger. This measurement is often used for ingredients that add flavor, such as sugar, salt, and spices. The amount can usually be adjusted according to taste. (A knife tip can be used to measure 3 to 4 pinches.)

10. To measure liquid, it is best to use a measuring cup. Be sure to hold it level, or stand it on a level surface, so that you will read the measurement correctly.

11. Although cooking is very easy, you must be very careful when working with sharp knives and utensils.

12. So you won't get a painful burn, always protect yourself from hot pot lids and handles, cake tins, or cookie sheets in use around the stove by using oven mitts or pot holders.

13. Be careful of steam when you are lifting the lid

of a pot, and of the boiling hot water when you are cooking noodles and vegetables.

The trick to chopping onions

After cutting off the end tips and peeling the onion, cut it into halves vertically from the stem to the root end. Place it on a cutting board with the flat, cut surface facing down.

Using a sharp knife, make several cuts from the center to the root end of the onion. *Do not* cut through the stem end, so that that end will help hold the onion together and make it easier to chop.

Cut the onion 2 or 3 times sideways (horizontally). Finally, holding the uncut stem end, chop down across the partial cuts to get little cubes of chopped onions. Finish up by chopping up the stem end.

Chopping onions is not easy, so don't give up if you don't do well the first time. Even a trick takes time to be mastered.

Is the egg still fresh?

In some of these recipes, you will be using eggs. Here are two ways to find out if the eggs you have are okay to use.

1. Fill a glass with water and place the egg into it. If the egg lies sideways on the bottom, it is fresh. This is because every egg has an air bubble at the rounded end. The older the egg is, the more air will have entered through the porous shell, making the air bubble larger. As the bubble grows, the egg will "swim" in the water and move up towards the surface.

2. A "smell test" will help you decide if a not-fresh egg is still usable. *Don't* hold the egg over your other ingredients, but over an empty cup. Crack it open and smell it. If it is not good anymore, it will smell like a stink bomb, and will have to be thrown out.

Help! I burned something!

This happens to even expert cooks, when something takes their minds off what they're doing for a moment. First, take the pot off the stove at once. (Don't forget to turn off the stove!) *Do not stir* the burned food, but carefully skim off what can still be saved. Fill the pot with water so that the burned food doesn't get hard and stick on the pot. It can be cleaned up later.

Recipes are meant to be altered

Sometimes a recipe will include something you do not like or cannot find in stores near you. Usually you can exchange it, or use a little more of the other ingredients to make up for leaving it out. Write down the change at once, so that you won't forget what you did. This way you can create your very own personal recipes by experimenting. Some of the tips included in this book are ideas for changing ingredients.

"A separate chapter about breakfast? What for?" The answer is simple. As you've probably been told, breakfast is the most important meal of the day. It has to give you energy for a long day at school, and it's not good to rush and just "wash down" a roll with juice or have cereal every morning for breakfast. So, here are some recipes that will wake up your taste buds and that can be put together quickly and easily. Then, we'll follow them up with some great new ideas for school snacks.

"Wake Up" Breakfast Kebobs

(4 servings, photo)

What You Need

2 T cream cheese with herbs
2 large slices whole grain
   bread
¼ cucumber
½ red pepper
1 big carrot
1 bunch radishes
3 oz chunk cheese (100 g)

How It's Done

1. Spread herbed cheese on one slice of whole grain bread, place the second slice on top of it and press together well.

2. Cut the sandwich into large cubes.

3. Wash the cucumber under warm, running water and dry it with a paper towel. Cut the cucumber into thick slices.

4. Cut open the pepper and remove the stem, seeds and white inner walls. Wash and dry it, then cut it into sections.

Have Ready

1 cutting board
1 peeler
1 kitchen knife
paper towel
skewers

5. Cut the ends off the carrot. Peel and cut it into thin slices.

6. Cut off the stems, leaves, and root of the radishes. Cut big radishes into halves, so that they can be skewered more easily.

7. Remove any rind from the chunk cheese, such as Gouda, and cut it into cubes.

8. Arrange the sandwich cubes onto the skewers or kebob sticks, alternating with vegetable slices and cheese.

Tip

You can make these nourishing breakfast kebobs using other vegetables, such as kohlrabi and zucchini, or with fruits as well!

Quick Cheese Rolls

(12 pieces)

What You Need

⅔ cup finely ground whole wheat flour (150 g)
1 t baking powder
1 t herb salt
4 oz cream cheese (125 g)
4 oz ricotta cheese (125 g)
1 egg
3 T whole wheat flour

Have Ready

1 baking sheet (greased)
1 pastry brush
1 big mixing bowl
1 electric mixer (with kneading hooks)
1 kitchen knife
1 cake rack

How It's Done

1. Put the flour, baking powder, herb salt and the cheeses into a big mixing bowl.

2. Add the egg and knead the ingredients with an electric mixer (first on slow, then high speed) until a smooth dough is created.

3. Sprinkle a little whole wheat flour on a baking board or the table top.

4. With your hands, mold the dough into a thick roll on the floured surface. Separate it into 12 portions about the same size.

5. To stop the dough from sticking to your fingers, rub your hands with some of the whole wheat flour. Roll each piece of dough into a round ball about 2 inches (5 cm) in diameter and place it on the greased baking sheet.

6. Set the sheet on the middle rack of the *pre-heated* oven.

Oven setting:
350°F (180°C)

Baking time:
15–20 minutes

7. Take the tray out of the oven (use thick pot holders, because the tray is very hot!). With a spatula, remove the rolls and place them on a rack to cool.

Muesli Bars *(photo)*

What You Need

½ cup water (125 mL)
2 cups honey (500 g)
1 cup crisp oatflakes (200 g)
1 cup crisp wheatflakes
  (200 g)
½ cup shredded dried coconut (100 g)
¼ cup sesame seeds (50 g)

1½ cups dried fruits, finely
  chopped (300 g)
2 pinches ground vanilla
1 t cinnamon
1 pinch salt
2 egg whites
2 egg yolks

Have Ready

1 small pot
1 large mixing bowl
1 wooden spoon
1 small bowl
1 fork
1 baking sheet
parchment paper
plastic wrap
    1 big knife
    1 rolling pin

How It's Done

1. Put the water and honey in a small pot. Stir and heat it up on the stove over medium heat until the honey is dissolved.

2. Place the oatflakes, wheatflakes, coconut, sesame seeds, dried fruits (such as apricots, apples, dates), vanilla, cinnamon, and salt into a large bowl. Mix all the ingredients well with a wooden spoon.

3. Add the honey-water and egg yolks to the dry mixture and stir until everything is evenly moistened. Let the muesli soak for 10 minutes.

4. Beat the two egg whites with an electric mixer or a fork until they are half stiff, then stir them into the muesli mix.

5. Cover the baking sheet with parchment paper and spread the muesli out on it. Cover it with plastic wrap and, with a rolling pin, press it tightly onto the baking sheet (see photo).

6. Peel off the plastic and place the baking sheet into the *pre-heated* oven.

**Oven setting:
325°F (160°C)**

**Baking time:
20–30 minutes**

7. Remove the sheet from the oven. Now you have one very large muesli cake. Cut the muesli into bars or squares while it is still hot and easy to cut.

Tip

An electric chopper can be used to cut the dried fruits into the small pieces needed.

Banana-Ham Sandwich *(1 serving, photo)*

What You Need

¼ cup cottage cheese (50 g)
2 slices whole grain bread
½ banana
½ t lemon juice
1 slice lean, cooked ham

Have Ready

1 cutting board
1 dinner knife

How It's Done

1. Spread the cottage cheese on the two slices of bread.

2. Cut the banana into slices and place them on one slice of bread.

3. Drip lemon juice onto the banana slices, so that they do not turn brown.

4. Put the slice of cooked ham on top of the banana slices.

5. Now add the second slice of bread, cottage-cheese-side down, like a lid to make the banana-ham sandwich.

Herbed Cheese Sandwich

(2 servings, photo)

What You Need

1 small carrot
4 oz light cream cheese
   (125 g)
1 T fresh herbs—parsley,
   chives, watercress
1 pinch salt
1 pinch pepper
1 pinch paprika, sweet
4 slices whole-grain bread

Have Ready

1 peeler
1 vegetable grater
1 small mixing bowl
1 wire whisk
1 dinner knife

How It's Done

1. Peel the carrot and then grate it, using the coarse side of the vegetable grater, into a small mixing bowl.

2. Add the cream cheese, fresh herbs, and spices. Blend everything together with a wire whisk.

3. Taste the herbed cheese mixture. If necessary, add some more of the spices to suit your taste.

4. Spread the cheese filling on 2 of the bread slices and place the other slices on top, and the sandwiches are ready to eat.

Tip

For a special touch, decorate the sandwiches with carrot stars.

Grain

All young cooks should know something about the different kinds of grain. For example, wheat and rye are primarily made into flour. Whole-grain flour comes from grinding whole kernels of grain, such as corn; while extract flour is ground from only the inner part. Multi-grain bread is, of course, made from a mixture of grains. Oats are used to make cereals like oatflakes or oatmeal. Millet is usually soaked in water before it is used in recipes. Corn and rice are eaten over much of the world as whole grains (rice grains are peeled, corn is unpeeled). So, as you can see, there are many ways to cook different grains or use them in baking. Here, especially for you, are some really great recipes using grain.

Oat-Dumpling Soup *(4-6 servings, photo)*

What You Need

½ stick butter, softened
  (60 g)
4 T finely ground oat flour
2 eggs
1 pinch salt
1 pinch pepper
1 pinch nutmeg
2 pinches bouillon powder
1 large carrot
¼ stalk celery
4 cups vegetable broth (1 L)

Have Ready

1 mixing bowl
1 electric mixer with wire
  whisk
1 peeler
1 vegetable grater
1 medium-large pot
2 teaspoons

How It's Done

1. Put the butter, the finely ground oat flour, and the eggs into a mixing bowl. Blend it with the mixer, set first on low and then on high speed, until a smooth batter is created.

2. Flavor the batter with salt, pepper, nutmeg and bouillon powder.

3. Set the oat-dumpling batter aside. Peel the carrot, and also the piece of celery to remove its tough outer "strings."

4. Shred the vegetables with the fine side of the vegetable grater and set them aside.

5. Pour the vegetable broth into a medium-large pot. Heat it up on the stove, at high setting, until it starts to boil. Reduce the heat to medium and add the prepared vegetables. Now it is time to make the dumplings.

6. It is best to make and drop the oat-dumplings into the broth with the help of 2 teaspoons. To do this, take some batter with one teaspoon and turn it, rolling the batter onto the second spoon, then drop the small mound of batter directly into the soup.

7. Cook the dumplings and the vegetables in the hot broth until well done, about 10 minutes.

Tip

It is easy to prepare a vegetable broth; just dissolve a vegetable bouillon cube in a cup (250 mL) of hot water. You can garnish the ready-to-serve soup with chopped parsley.

Sweet Millet Soufflé *(4-6 servings, photo)*

What You Need

1 cup millet (200 g)
2 cups milk (500 mL)
2 T honey
3 T sesame seeds
3 T chopped almonds
½ t ground cinnamon
3 egg yolks
2 cups fruit—pitted cherries, peaches, apples (500 g)
3 egg whites
butter, to grease soufflé dish

Have Ready

1 sieve
1 medium-large pot with lid
1 deep mixing bowl
1 electric mixer with wire whisk
1 wooden spoon
1 soufflé dish
1 pastry brush
1 kitchen knife

How It's Done

1. Put the millet into a sieve and wash it under warm, running water.

2. Put the washed millet together with the milk into a pot. Heat it up over high heat until it is boiling.

3. Take the boiling millet off the stove and let it sit for 20 minutes.

4. Stir the honey, sesame seeds, chopped almonds, and cinnamon into the millet.

5. Add one egg yolk after another, blending them thoroughly each time.

6. Prepare the fruits. (If you use the larger fruits, like peaches or apples, you will need to peel and slice or cube them for use.)

7. Beat the egg white until stiff in a deep mixing bowl, with the electric mixer set on high, so that a cut with a knife remains visible.

8. With the ladle, carefully fold the stiff egg white into the millet batter.

9. Grease the soufflé dish with a little butter and pour or spoon the batter into it.

10. Put the soufflé dish on the middle rack in the *pre-heated* oven. Cook as follows and it will be ready to serve.

Oven setting:
350°F (175°C)

Baking time:
30 minutes

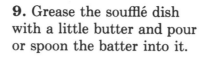

Tip

Millet can be found in many health food stores. A vanilla sauce goes especially well with this sweet millet soufflé. Use colorful fruit, such as kiwi, strawberries and cherries, to decorate the soufflé.

Vanilla Sauce

(4–6 servings)

What You Need

1 cup milk (250 mL)
5 pinches ground vanilla
3 T finely ground whole-wheat flour (40 g)
1 egg yolk
2 T honey
1 t lemon juice
1 pinch salt
1 cup whipping cream (250 mL)

Have Ready

1 pot
1 wire whisk
1 cup

How It's Done

1. Put the milk, ground vanilla, and whole-wheat flour into a pot. Heat it up on the stove on high heat until it is boiling. Important: You will have to stir it continuously with the wire whisk so that it doesn't burn.

2. Take the pot off the stove. Help the milk mix to cool a bit by continuing to stir it for a minute.

3. In a cup, mix the egg yolk with the honey, lemon juice, pinch of salt, and 3 tablespoons of the hot milk mix.

4. Stir the egg mixture into the pot with the rest of the hot milk.

5. Finally, add the whipping cream. Stir everything again thoroughly, and your vanilla sauce is ready.

Apple Fritters

(4 servings, photo)

What You Need

1 cup finely ground whole-wheat flour (250 g)
1 pinch salt
3 eggs
1 cup milk (250 mL)
3 apples
2 T whole-wheat flour (30 g)
2 pinches baking powder
2 T salad oil, to fry the fritters

Have Ready

1 large mixing bowl
1 small mixing bowl
1 cup, to separate eggs
1 electric mixer with whisk
   or
1 wire whisk
1 kitchen scale
1 measuring cup
1 peeler
1 cutting board
1 tablespoon
2 cooking spatulas
1 wooden spoon
1 paper towel

How It's Done

1. Put the cup of flour in a large mixing bowl and add the pinch of salt.

2. Now separate the three eggs. To do this, use a cup and crack each egg open by hitting it sharply against the rim. Then, holding the cracked egg above the cup, carefully move the egg yolk from one half-shell to the other. Let the egg white run into the cup, until the yolk is completely separated from the egg white.

3. Add the egg yolk to the flour. Put the egg white into the small mixing bowl.

4. Add the milk to the flour and blend everything well with the electric mixer, first at low speed and then at high, until the batter is smooth.

5. Let the batter sit for ½ hour.

6. In the meantime, peel the apples, cut them into 4 pieces and remove the cores. Cut each of the quarter pieces lengthwise into small slices.

7. Carefully fold the apple slices into the batter (do not wait too long as the cut apples will turn brown quickly).

8. Mix the remaining flour with the baking powder and add it to the batter.

9. Beat the egg white with the mixer until it is so stiff that a cut made with a knife remains visible.

10. Carefully fold the egg white into the batter.

11. Use a tablespoon to spoon the batter into the hot oil (about 2 tablespoons for each of 4 fritters) in the frying pan.

12. When the underside of the apple fritters are golden yellow, turn them over using two spatulas. Let them cook until they are fried a golden yellow on that side too. Place the fritters on a paper towel to drain for a moment before serving.

Tip

The fritters taste good with cinnamon and sugar, or with maple syrup.

Noodles

What is life without noodles! There is really no substitute for a real spaghetti dinner. Besides, noodles are very quick and easy to cook. All you need to do is boil water. What's best about noodles is you can also make them fresh yourself! It's not difficult at all. Even colorful noodles are foolproof. Instead of cooking them in water, you simply cook them in vegetable juice: that is, in spinach juice if you want green noodles; in beet juice if you want them to be red. And if you feel like eating something sweet, noodles are great for that, too. Why don't you just go ahead and try your own favorite noodle recipe right now.

Homemade Noodles *(photo)*

What You Need

3¾ cups finely ground
    whole-wheat flour (500 g)
5 eggs
3–4 T water or milk
1 pinch salt

Have Ready

1 large mixing bowl
1 cup
1 wooden spoon
1 rolling pin
1 kitchen knife *or*
1 dough cutter (roller)

How It's Done

1. Pour the flour into a large bowl. Make a "pocket" in the middle of the flour.

2. Break the eggs one by one into a cup. Be careful not to let any shells fall into the cup. Put the eggs into the depression you made in the flour.

3. With a wooden spoon, mix the eggs into the flour. Stir the water or milk and the salt into the flour mixture.

4. When all the ingredients are well mixed, knead the dough thoroughly with your hands. The dough has to be completely smooth and elastic before you stop.

5. When finished, let the dough sit for 30 minutes. Then, with a rolling pin, roll the dough out as thinly as possible onto a board covered with flour or on the kitchen table.

6. Cut it into strips about ¼ inch (½ cm) wide with a sharp kitchen knife or roller. You can also roll out small triangles, strips, or squares for "bows" as shown.

7. Now the noodles have to dry for 30 minutes. The dried noodles can be kept a couple of days, if you cannot use them all up immediately.

Tip

Rolling out the dough is easier if you divide it beforehand into 4 or 5 portions. You can tint the dough different colors by substituting some kind of vegetable juice (beet, spinach) for the water or milk in the recipe. Note: To make yellow, saffron noodles, put the saffron in lukewarm water first, and it will turn a beautiful yellow.

Spaghetti with Meat Sauce

(4 servings, photo)

What You Need

For the Sauce

1 large onion
½ lb chopped meat (250 g)
1 T butter or margarine
3 T tomato paste
½ cup warm water (125 mL)
¼ t salt
¼ t ground pepper
¼ t oregano

To Cook the Noodles

2 qts water (2 L)
2 t salt
½ t salad oil
1 lb spaghetti (250 g)
⅓ cup grated cheese (100 g)

Have Ready

1 sharp knife
1 small cutting board
1 frying pan
1 cooking spatula
1 tablespoon
1 small mixing bowl
1 large pot
1 wooden spoon
1 sieve

How It's Done

1. Peel the onion and chop it finely.

2. Put the butter or margarine in the frying pan. Let it melt on the stove on high heat.

3. Put the chopped meat into the hot fat. Quickly break it up with the spatula. Turn the heat down and brown the meat on all sides over medium heat until it becomes crumbly.

4. Add the chopped onions and fry until they turn "glassy," at the same time stirring the meat again and again so that it doesn't burn.

5. Combine the tomato paste with the warm water and pour it over the chopped meat.

6. Now spice up the sauce with salt, pepper, and oregano.

7. Let the sauce come to a boil briefly, then turn the heat to low to simmer for 8 minutes.

8. In the meantime, put the water together with the salt and oil into a big pot. Heat it up, on high, until boiling.

9. When the water boils, carefully place the spaghetti in the pot. With a wooden spoon, push any noodles which stick out down into the water.

10. Cook the spaghetti noodles until they are soft, about 10 minutes.

11. Carefully, pour the cooked noodles into a colander, rinse them briefly under warm, running water. Let them drain well.

12. Spread the noodles on a plate, pour the meat sauce on top. Sprinkle with grated cheese.

Easy Cheese Noodles

(4 servings)

What You Need

To Cook the Noodles

2 qts water (2 L)
1 pinch salt
1 T salad oil
1 lb noodles, homemade, if possible (500 g)

For the Sauce

¾ stick butter (100 g)
1 cup whipping cream (250 mL)
¾ cup freshly grated cheese (200 g)
salt and pepper to taste

Have Ready

1 large pot
1 wooden spoon
1 colander

How It's Done

1. Put the water with the salt and oil into a large pot. Turn the heat to high until it starts to boil.

2. Carefully pour the noodles into the boiling water. Stir with the wooden spoon to separate them.

3. Turn the heat down. Cook the noodles over very low heat for about 10 minutes.

4. Pour the noodles into a colander. Let the noodles drain.

5. Put the drained noodles back in the pot and place it on the stove.

6. Add the butter to the noodles and let it melt on low heat.

7. Pour the whipping cream onto the noodles, and keep stirring carefully so that nothing burns.

8. Finally, add the grated cheese to the noodle mix. Stir slowly until the cheese is melted and thoroughly mixed with the noodles.

9. Take the pot off the stove and taste the cheese noodles. If you want, you can add a light sprinkling of salt and pepper for flavor.

Vegetables

As you probably already know, the combination and variety of foods you eat is very important. In addition to many other substances, the body needs vitamins and minerals to help it grow and to keep you from getting sick. Vegetables have lots of vitamins and minerals. In the summer, when vegetables grow everywhere and are harvested, you can sometimes eat raw carrots, cucumbers and radishes fresh from the garden. That's when they are best, and make really great salads. One quick tip: Always wash vegetables and salad makings before you prepare them. You do this by scrubbing them with a vegetable brush or rinsing them quickly under cold, running water. Do not let the vegetables sit in standing (not running) water or some of the vitamins and minerals will seep out into the water and end up going down the drain.
And they don't do *you* any good down there!

Fruited Cabbage Salad

(4 servings, photo)

What You Need

3 carrots
¼ medium cabbage
4 sweet apples
1 cup raisins
8–10 T orange juice
3 T lemon juice

Have Ready

1 vegetable brush
1 peeler
1 carving knife
1 vegetable grater
paper towel
1 mixing bowl
1 wooden spoon

How It's Done

1. Cut the stems and root ends off the carrots. Scrub the carrots with the vegetable brush under cold, running water.

2. Peel the carrots and rasp them using the coarse side of the vegetable grater.

3. Remove the outer leaves of the cabbage. Rinse and dry them, then shred them, using the slicer part of the vegetable grater, into fine strips. (Watch out for your fingers. The cabbage can quickly slip out of your hand.)

4. Wash the apples under warm, running water and dry them. Cut them into 4 pieces, remove the cores, and rasp the apples, peel and all, with the coarse side of the vegetable grater.

5. Mix the carrots with the white cabbage and the apples in a bowl.

6. Add the raisins and the orange and lemon juices, and mix everything together thoroughly.

Tip

This salad tastes especially good after it has been allowed to sit for a while so that the flavors blend. Use oranges instead of carrots if you want a change. Peel and cut the oranges into small pieces and add them to the salad. In this case, you would leave out the orange juice.

Tomato-Cucumber Boats

(4 servings, photo)

What You Need

4 tomatoes
1 salad cucumber
8 toothpicks

Have Ready

paper towel
1 peeler
1 kitchen knife
1 small cutting board

How It's Done

1. Wash the tomatoes thoroughly. Dry and cut them into 4 quarters.

2. Wash the salad cucumber, too, then dry it and cut it into 8 slices about ¼ inch (½ cm) thick.

3. Cut each slice into a triangle.

4. Pierce the cucumber triangle with a toothpick and stick it onto the tomato quarter like a sail to make the boat.

Broccoli Cake

(6 servings)

What You Need

1 10 oz pkg biscuit dough, frozen (300 g)
2 lb broccoli, fresh or frozen (1 kg)
1 qt water (1 L)
1 t salt
3 T ground almonds
½ cup chunk cheese, grated (100 g)
3 eggs
1 cup sour cream (225 g)
1 pinch salt
1 pinch paprika

Have Ready

1 rolling pin
1 springform pan, about 10 inches (26 cm) diameter
1 kitchen knife
1 large pot
1 skimming ladle
1 colander
1 cup
1 mixing bowl
1 wire whisk

How It's Done

1. Take the frozen biscuit dough out of the package and let it defrost at room temperature.

2. In the meantime, prepare the broccoli. With fresh broccoli, cut the small, floret stems off of the main stalk. Discard the tough lower stem. Wash the stems and floret heads under running water. Let them drain. Prepare the frozen broccoli according to the instructions on the package.

3. Place the water and teaspoon of salt into a pot. Set the stove heat to high, and bring the water to a boil. Put the prepared broccoli into the boiling salt water and cook it for 15 minutes over medium heat. Then carefully take the broccoli out of the pot with a skimming ladle or slotted spoon and let it drain in a colander.

4. Roll out the puff-pastry dough layers. Place them on top of each other on a working surface sprinkled with flour and roll them out with a rolling pin. Place the bottom part of the springform pan on the rolled-out dough and cut around the outer edge with a knife. Cover the bottom of the pan with this round dough layer and cover the sides of the springform pan with strips of the leftover dough pieces, carefully pressing them against the bottom.

5. Sprinkle the ground almonds over the dough bottom and place the broccoli on it.

6. Sprinkle the ground cheese over the broccoli.

7. Break the eggs carefully one after another over a cup and then put them into a mixing bowl. Whip the eggs with a wire whisk and then blend in the sour cream.

8. Spice the egg mixture with salt, pepper, and paprika. Pour it into the broccoli cake pan, and bake until done.

Oven setting:
400°F (200°C)

Baking time:
40 minutes

Tip

Do not knead puff pastry dough or it will not rise. You can use leftover dough pieces, however, by putting them on top of each other and rolling them out again.

Egg-Mushrooms in Spinach Bed *(photo)*

What You Need

1 cup water
2 eggs
9 oz pkg creamed spinach, frozen (300 g)
1 firm tomato
mayonnaise, in decorating tube

Have Ready

1 egg piercer
2 small pots
1 tablespoon
paper towel
1 wooden spoon
1 carving knife

How It's Done

1. Bring the water to a boil in a small pot on the stove (high heat).

2. Pierce the eggs on the blunt (rounded) end with an egg piercer. This will allow the air to escape while they are being cooked and the eggs will not burst.

3. Carefully place each of the eggs in turn in a spoon and lower them into the boiling water. Turn the heat down to low and cook the eggs for 10 minutes.

4. In the meantime, put the frozen spinach into a second pot and let it defrost over low heat. Cook it following the instructions on the spinach package.

5. Take the pot with the eggs off the stove. Carefully pour off the hot water. Rinse the eggs under cold water briefly to stop the cooking process and cool the eggs for handling.

6. Peel the eggs and cut a small slice off of the blunt end. This will make the eggs stand up better.

7. Wash the tomato under cold, running water. Dry it with a paper towel, and cut it into halves.

8. With a teaspoon, scoop out all the seeds, hollowing out the tomato halves. Place them onto the eggs, like hats.

9. For two servings, spoon half of the spinach onto each plate and place one of the egg-mushrooms in the middle.

10. Using a decorating tube, decorate the "mushroom caps" with mayonnaise dots so that they really look like toadstools.

Throughout the year, you can eat the most wonderful fruits whenever and as many as you want. It's no wonder that, with such a big choice available, a great many cooking and baking recipes include fruits. Fresh fruits are not only delicious but, like vegetables, they contain many of the vitamins and minerals your body needs to keep you healthy. Also, they are so naturally sweet that you hardly need to add any sugar at all. Whenever eating fruits such as apples or peaches whole, you should eat them without peeling. Right underneath the peel are the nutrients that make the fruit so healthy to eat and you don't want to lose that. Always remember, though, to wash it off first. Now that I've stirred up your appetite, let's go on to the recipes.

Crunchy Apple Dish *(4 servings, photo)*

What You Need

1 T butter
1 T oatflakes
1 cup whipping cream
   (250 mL)
1 lb apples (400 g)
⅓ cup chopped almonds
   (100 g)
2 t honey
1 pinch cinnamon

Have Ready

1 pan
1 cooking spatula
1 flat plate
1 electric mixer with whisk
paper towel
      1 kitchen knife
         1 vegetable grater
            1 wooden spoon

How It's Done

1. Let the butter melt in a pan on the stove over middle heat.

2. Add the oatflakes to the melted butter and roast them until they are crispy. Be sure to stir them constantly so that they do not burn. Pour the golden-brown, roasted oatflakes onto a plate to cool.

3. Pour the whipping cream into a bowl. Beat it stiff with the mixer.

4. Wash the apples under hot, running water and wipe them dry with the paper towel.

5. Cut the washed apples into 4 quarters and cut out the cores. Grate the apple pieces coarsely with a vegetable grater, add them to the whipping cream and fold them in carefully.

6. Add the chopped almonds to the apple dish and carefully fold them in, too.

7. Spice the apple dish with honey and cinnamon.

8. Spoon portions into a bowl and sprinkle with the roasted oatflakes. You have to serve and eat the "crispy" apple dish immediately, before the oatflakes get soft.

Fruit Salad

(2 servings)

What You Need

1 orange
1 banana
1 apple
1 t lemon juice
1 T sugar or honey

Have Ready

1 kitchen knife
1 peeler
1 cutting board
1 bowl
1 spoon

How It's Done

1. Peel the orange, divide it into sections and cut the orange sections into little pieces. Put the pieces into a bowl.

2. Peel the banana and cut it into halves lengthwise. Cut the banana halves into slices and put them into the bowl carefully mixing them with the orange pieces.

3. Wash the apple, peel it, and cut it into 8 pieces. Remove the core, then cut the apple sections into fine slices and add them to the bowl.

4. Pour the lemon juice over the fruits, so that the bananas and apples do not turn brown.

5. Add the sugar or honey and mix everything together. Taste it to see if the fruit salad is sweet enough. If not, add a little more honey or sugar. If too sweet, add a little more lemon juice.

Tip

For a change, you can also add a handful of grapes, a cut-up pear, or cherry halves to the fruit salad. This recipe also tastes great with peaches instead of oranges.

Apple Soup with Kiwi

(4-6 servings, photo)

What You Need

1 lb apples (500 g)
2 cups water (500 mL)
1 T cornstarch
3 T water
¼ cup sugar (50 g)
1 T lemon juice
4 kiwis

Have Ready

1 knife
1 chopping board
1 medium-sized pot with lid
1 sieve
1 spoon
1 measuring cup
1 cup
1 small wire whisk

How It's Done

1. Wash the apples under hot, running water, and cut them into 4 quarters. Remove the cores.

2. Put the apples and 2 cups of water into a pot. Steam them over medium heat in the closed pot until they are soft.

3. Place a sieve over a large measuring cup. Spoon the steamed apples into it and push them through the sieve with a spoon.

4. Now see how much apple sauce you have. If there is less than 1 quart of the sauce, add water until you have 1 quart.

5. Pour the apple sauce back into the pot and bring it to a boil on the stove at the highest level heat. Careful, the apple soup may spatter!

6. Mix the cornstarch in a cup with 3 tablespoons of cold water until it is smooth. Slowly add it to the boiling soup. It is very important to keep stirring so that no lumps will form. As soon as the apple soup has come to a boil again, remove it from the stove.

7. Add the sugar and lemon juice to the apple soup and stir well. Take a little bit on the end of a spoon and taste it. Be careful, it may still be hot. Add more sugar or lemon juice if necessary.

8. Peel the kiwi fruits and slice them. Put the kiwi slices into the soup, stir it one more time, and it is ready to eat. Apple-kiwi soup can be served hot or cold.

Do you get tired of being served soda, hot chocolate, or lemonade to drink every time you are visiting someone? Yet it is so easy to make delicious and different hot or cold drinks that really wake up your taste buds. There are all kinds of shakes, floats, punches, and fruit juice thirst quenchers to try. And not only can you use whatever ingredients you like, you can also let yourself go on the decorations and really get your guests to smile. Here are some ideas to get you started. Pretty soon you'll be serving up the greatest soft drinks in the neighborhood!

Pineapple Yogurt Shake

(1 serving, photo)

What You Need

2 pineapple slices, canned
1 t lemon juice
1 t sugar
2 T vanilla ice cream
½ cup yogurt (150 g)
2 T whipping cream, whipped stiff

Have Ready

1 electric mixer
1 high mixing bowl
1 wire whisk
1 thick straw

How It's Done

1. Put the pineapple slices, lemon juice and sugar into a high bowl and blend the ingredients with a mixer.

2. With the whisk, stir the vanilla ice cream and the yogurt thoroughly into the pineapple mix.

3. Fold the stiffly whipped cream into the yogurt shake.

4. Pour the beverage immediately into a high glass and serve it with a thick straw.

Apricot Flip

(4 servings, photo)

What You Need

4 oz apricots with juice,
 canned (113 g)
2 cups buttermilk (500 mL)

Have Ready

1 large, high mixing bowl
1 electric mixer (with
 blender attachment)
1 wire whisk

How It's Done

1. Put the canned apricots
and juice into a bowl and
blend them using the mixer
with blender attachment.

2. Add the buttermilk to it
and thoroughly mix
everything.

3. Put the apricot flip into
the refrigerator for half an
hour. Pour the beverage into
glasses to serve.

Tip

Of course, like the other
recipes, you can use all
different kinds of fruits
to make a flip. Try it
with peaches.

Hot Spiced Cup

(6 servings, photo)

What You Need

2 qt fruit juice—apple,
   cherry, orange (2 L)
1 T honey
½ t ground cinnamon
2 pinches ground cloves
2 T lemon juice

Have Ready

1 large pot
1 wooden spoon
6 cups or heat-resistant
   glasses

How It's Done

1. Pour the juice (such as apple, cherry or orange) into a pot and slowly warm it up on medium heat.

2. As soon as the juice begins to boil, immediately take it off the stove.

3. Add the honey, the spices, and the lemon juice. Stir, then let the fruit-juice cup stand briefly (about 5 minutes).

4. Test the hot punch by tasting it and adding more of some ingredient if needed. Serve in cups or heat-resistant glasses.

Lemon Tea

(6 servings, photo)

What You Need

1 qt rosehip or black tea (1 L)
1 qt cherry, berry or currant
  juice (1 L)
2 cup seltzer water (500 mL)
1 T lemon juice
ice cubes

Have Ready

1 large bowl *or*
1 large glass pitcher
1 wooden spoon

How It's Done

1. Mix the tea, fruit juice,
and seltzer water in a large
bowl or glass pitcher.

2. Add the lemon juice and
the ice cubes to taste.

Tip

Make sure the tea, juice
and seltzer water are
well chilled. The lemon
tea then tastes espe-
cially good.

Tingly Orange Punch *(4 servings, photo)*

What You Need

4 oranges
1 qt apple juice (1 L)
1½ cup seltzer water (⅓ L)

Have Ready

1 cutting board
1 peeler
1 glass pitcher

How It's Done

1. Peel the oranges and divide them into sections. Using a cutting board and knife, slice the sections into small pieces.

2. Put the orange pieces into a glass pitcher and put it in the refrigerator for about 15 minutes to chill.

3. Add the apple juice and the seltzer water, and stir everything together thoroughly.

Tip

The apple juice and seltzer water should also be well chilled, so that the punch is very cold and refreshing. If it is especially hot outside, you can also add some ice cubes, or put a scoop of vanilla ice cream into each glass for a refreshing orange float!

Banana Milkshake *(4 servings, photo)*

What You Need

2 bananas
2 T lemon juice
1 qt milk (1 L)
2 t vanilla sugar

Have Ready

1 cutting board
1 knife
1 mixer *or*
1 hand-operated blender *or*
1 fork

How It's Done

1. Peel the bananas and cut them into small pieces.

2. Put the banana pieces and the lemon juice into a mixer and blend them well.

3. Then add the milk and vanilla sugar and blend everything together well before serving.

Tip

It doesn't always have to be bananas! You can use other fruits (like strawberries, blueberries, raspberries, etc.). For the photograph, we prepared a *strawberry* milkshake instead of banana. Did you notice?

What do you think about cooking a whole menu for the guests at your next birthday party? With what you have already learned from this book, it would be no problem at all. Your friends would be bowled over, when you surprise them with food you made yourself. Here are some more recipes to try, even one for pizza. But, before you start cooking for a party, you will need to plan everything in advance. First, you will need to know how many guests will be coming so that you do not buy too much or too few groceries for the recipes. Have fun!

Baked Banana Boats *(2 servings, photo)*

What You Need

1 banana
1 T lemon juice
6 T or squares vanilla ice
  cream
½ T chocolate sprinkles
fruit slices (optional)

Have Ready

paper towel
1 cutting board
1 kitchen knife
1 oven-proof dish
1 pastry brush
1 tablespoon
2 plates

How It's Done

1. Wash the banana thoroughly under cold, running water and dry it with a paper towel.

2. Cut the unpeeled banana down the middle lengthwise into halves and place them, with the cut surface facing upwards, into the dish.

3. Use a pastry brush to coat the cut surfaces of the banana halves with lemon juice so they will not turn brown.

4. Slide the oven-proof dish into the *pre-heated* oven.

Oven setting:
400°F (200°C)

Baking time:
about 5–10 minutes

5. Place one baked banana half on each plate. Top them with three large spoonsful or squares of vanilla ice cream.

6. Finally, drop chocolate or other decorative sprinkles onto the banana boats. If you want to, you can decorate them with berries and fruit slices, too.

43

Honeyspice Cookies *(2 servings, photo)*

What You Need

For the Dough

⅔ cup honey (250 g)
⅓ cup sugar (100 g)
2 t vanilla sugar
1 egg
1 t cinnamon
2 pinches ground cloves
2 pinches ground nutmeg
¼ t lemon flavoring
1 t rum flavoring
4 cups all-purpose flour
  (500 g)
1½ T baking powder
2 T evaporated milk

For the Garnish

almonds, chopped
almonds, halved
pistachio nuts, chopped
pistachio nuts, halved
candied fruit or jam
raisins
colored sugar
chocolate sprinkles
candy sprinkles
sugar flowers
small candies

Have Ready

1 mixing bowl
1 wooden spoon
tracing paper
1 pencil
1 rolling pin
1 cookie sheet, greased
1 cake rack
1 pastry brush

How It's Done

1. *For the dough*, put the honey, sugar, vanilla sugar, egg, cinnamon, cloves, nutmeg, lemon and rum flavorings into a big bowl. Mix the ingredients together thoroughly.

2. Mix the flour and baking powder together. Stir one third of it into the honey mixture.

3. Put the dough on the table. Knead the remaining flour into it with your hands.

4. Place tracing paper over the Honeyspice couple shown. Outline the two figures separately on the paper. Cut out the stencils.

5. Roll the dough out to about ¼ inch (½ cm) thick. Place the paper stencils on the dough. Cut out the two figures.

6. Place the Honeyspices on a well-greased cookie sheet. Brush them with evaporated milk. Press candied cherries, almonds, raisins, and pistachio nuts into the dough.

7. Slide the cookie sheet into the *pre-heated* oven.

Oven setting:
350–400°F (175–200°C)

Baking time:
about 25 minutes

8. *To garnish*, decorate with colored sugar and chocolate sprinkles. Use some jam or icing on a pastry brush to "glue" sugar flowers and small candies to the baked figures.

Pizza Napoli *(4 servings, photo)*

What You Need

For the Dough

1¾ cup all-purpose flour
   (350 g)
1 pkg dry baking yeast
¾ cup lukewarm milk
   (200 mL)
1 t salt
1 T butter (to grease baking
   sheet)

For the Topping

4 T salad oil
8 T tomato ketchup
4 cups whole tomatoes,
   canned (850 mL)
2 cups mushrooms, canned
   (425 mL)
2 onions
1 t salt

1 t pepper
1 t oregano
12 slices salami
¼ cup grated cheese (100 g)

Have Ready

2 large bowls
1 mixer, with kneading
   hooks
1 baking tin
1 rolling pin
1 small cup
1 pastry brush
1 tablespoon
1 sieve
1 carving knife
1 kitchen board

How It's Done

1. Put the flour into a large bowl and mix it well with the yeast. Add the salt, butter, and milk and blend everything together thoroughly with the electric mixer, using the kneading hooks.

2. Put the dough on a table-top or counter. Knead it with your hands until it becomes smooth.

3. Form it into a ball and let the dough sit at room temperature until it has "risen" (gotten bigger).

4. Spread butter evenly on the baking sheet and put the ball of dough on the greased sheet.

5. Roll the dough out with a rolling pin so that the whole sheet is covered with a thin layer of dough.

6. Mix the oil and tomato ketchup in a small cup and, using a pastry brush, coat the dough.

7. Next, spoon the tomatoes out of the can and cut them into big cubes.

8. Drain the mushrooms well in a sieve and cut them into slices.

9. Prepare the onions by removing their outer skins and cutting them into slices.

10. Spread the tomato pieces, the mushrooms, and the onion slices out on the dough.

11. Sprinkle the pizza with salt, pepper, and oregano.

12. Cover the top of the pizza with the salami slices and the grated cheese.

13. Now slide the baking sheet onto the middle rack of the *pre-heated* oven to bake.

Oven setting:
400°F (200°C)

Baking time:
about 30 minutes

Index